Hey there, I hope you are doing fine. This is like a dream project for me. I always wanted to write a book but never thought that I would end up writing this one. This book is ideal for students or anyone who wants to invest money. This book will cover my journey as a student and an investor. I am currently a research scholar, and I started investing in the stock market as a hobby. In this book, I will be writing down my personal experience with the stock market and very basic concepts that can help you start your investment journey.

When I look around, I see many people still unaware of the potential of investment, especially in the stock market. I will try to explain in simple terms and I am sure you will not regret reading this.

Thank you

Contents:

1) Who should read?

2) The Indian stock market, my initial days.

3) Is this the perfect time?

4) Why should you even care about investment?

5) Do you think it is still risky?

6) Other investment options

7) Understanding investment in equity

8) Freedom of control

9) The 1 year long experiment.

Who should read?

Everyone should read. Reading enhances our knowledge, improves our vocabulary, and sharpens our critical thinking skills. It helps us focus better, boosts our empathy, and fuels our creativity. Despite these benefits, many people read less today because of digital distractions and busy schedules. If this trend continues, we might face reduced cognitive abilities, limited perspectives, and shorter attention spans. So, yes, everyone should read, especially when it comes to learning about something as important as investing.

If you're in your 20s, 30s, or even 40s, and all your money is just sitting in a bank account without being invested, this book is for you. If you've recently heard about the stock market and are considering starting your investment journey, you've picked up the right book. If you have some savings and are looking for a place to invest, I believe this book will give you a good idea of where to start. As someone from a science background, I don't claim to be an expert writer. You might find some mistakes in my writing, but my goal is to communicate and encourage you to start investing. So, read on, even if it's just to learn something new.

In this book, we'll cover the basics of investing. If you've been investing for a few years, you might already know some of this information. But for those who are just starting, these basics are essential.

Let's understand this with a simple example:

Jaya is a final-year graduate student. After completing her studies, she gets a job and starts earning Rs. 30,000 per month. She's thrilled and often helps out her family. Coming from a middle-class background, she doesn't have to worry too much about money. After all her expenses, Jaya saves around 60% of her salary, which is Rs. 18,000 per month. She plans to work for three more years and then hopes to go abroad for higher studies.

This sounds pretty good. Jaya is clear about her future plans and is already saving money for them. However, here's where a small change could make a big difference. If Jaya simply keeps saving Rs. 18,000 each month in her bank account, she'll have about Rs. 6.8 lakhs after three years, assuming the bank gives an annual return of at least 5%.

Now, imagine if Jaya reads this book and learns about different ways of investing. She decides to invest in a safe option like a mutual fund. Let's assume she starts investing Rs. 18,000 monthly in a mutual fund with an expected annual return of 12%. By the end of three years, she would have around Rs. 7.7 lakhs. The mutual fund, with a higher return, would give her a significantly greater amount compared to just saving in a bank account. Jaya could have made an extra Rs. 90,000 after three years by choosing a different investment option. That's the power of investing wisely!

Let's take another example to understand this better:

Moti is a 26-year-old guy who works in a company and earns around Rs. 50,000 monthly. He has worked there for the last two years and dreams of buying a new bike. Moti lives in Bangalore, where rent takes a significant chunk of his earnings. He also enjoys spending time with his friends, and as a result, he struggles to save money. Despite wanting to save, he always feels far from achieving his dream of buying that bike.

One day, Moti comes across this book and learns about a financial product called an ETF (Exchange-Traded Fund). After doing some research, he decided to start investing Rs. 5,000 every month in an ETF. He keeps investing this amount for two straight years. The ETF Moti invested in gives a return of 30% per year, and at the end of two years, he finds himself with an extra Rs. 45,000. With this additional money, Moti finally gets his dream bike!

For Moti, Rs. 5,000 wasn't a huge amount, but he never realized that such a small, consistent investment could bring him closer to his dream.

These examples of Jaya and Moti show how important it is to understand and choose the right investment options. Both of them started with small amounts, but by choosing different paths for their money, they achieved their goals more effectively. If you feel you're new to the world of investments, don't worry. This book is here to guide you.

The stock market and other investment avenues might seem overwhelming at first, but they are not as complicated as they appear. With the right knowledge and a bit of patience, anyone can start their investment journey. The key is to understand your goals, assess how much risk you're willing to take, and choose the right investments accordingly.

You might wonder why investing is so important. Why not just keep your money in a savings account? The answer is simple: inflation. Inflation means that the prices of goods and services go up over time. If your money is just sitting in a bank account with a low-interest rate, it's not growing enough to keep up with inflation. Essentially, you're losing money over time because your purchasing power decreases.

Investing allows your money to grow at a rate that can outpace inflation. Over the long term, investments like mutual funds, ETFs, and even stocks can provide returns that significantly enhance your wealth. This growth helps you meet your future financial goals, whether it's buying a home, funding education, or saving for retirement.

Many people are afraid to invest because they don't want to lose their hard-earned money. This fear is natural, but it shouldn't stop you from exploring investment options. Remember, investing doesn't mean you have to put all your money into the stock market. There are many safe options like government bonds, fixed deposits, and mutual funds that can offer better returns than a regular savings account without taking too much risk.

Start small. Even a small investment can make a big difference over time, thanks to the power of compounding. Compounding means earning returns on both your initial investment and the returns that investment has already generated. This snowball effect can lead to significant growth over time.

Everyone makes mistakes, especially when they're starting out. I've made my share of mistakes too, but each one taught me something valuable about investing. Don't be afraid to make mistakes; instead, see them as learning opportunities. By reading this book, you'll hopefully avoid some of the mistakes I made and start your investment journey on a stronger footing.

As you move forward, remember that investing is a journey, not a destination. It's about consistently making smart decisions and learning along the way. By the time you finish this book, you'll have a clearer understanding of how to start investing, where to put your money, and how to grow your wealth over time. I hope this book inspires you to take control of your financial future.

Happy reading and happy investing!

Diversifying your investments across sectors and industries
can help reduce risk and increase stability.

The Indian stock market, my initial days

When you think about "The Stock Market," you might imagine a scene straight out of a movie: someone sitting in front of multiple screens, intently analyzing charts with red and green lines moving up and down. The stock market often evokes images of a fast-paced, high-risk environment where fortunes can be made or lost in seconds. This perception isn't entirely wrong, but it's only a small part of a much bigger picture.

In reality, investing in the stock market today can be straightforward and accessible to anyone with a smartphone and an internet connection. You don't need a massive amount of money or an economics degree to get started. With the right knowledge and tools, anyone can become an investor and participate in the potential growth of businesses worldwide. To understand the stock market, let's break it down into two fundamental components: "stock" and "market." The stock market is, at its core, a place where people buy and sell stocks. But what exactly are stocks?

Stocks, also known as shares or equities, represent ownership in a company. When you purchase a stock, you essentially buy a small piece of that company, making you a shareholder. This means that you have a claim on a portion of the company's assets and earnings. For example, imagine you own stock in a company that produces smartphones, bakes delicious pastries or manufactures your favorite sneakers. By purchasing these companies' stocks, you're investing in their potential for growth and success. If the company performs well and its value increases, the value of your stocks may also rise, allowing you to sell them at a profit. Conversely, if the company doesn't do well, the value of your stocks might decrease, and you could sell them at a loss. In essence, the stock market allows you to invest in businesses you believe in and share in their success or failure.

As you delve deeper into the world of investing, you'll encounter terms like "equities," "capital," "index," and many others. These terms might seem daunting at first, but they are just the language of the stock market. As you continue reading, I'll try to use simple terms to explain these concepts. It's essential to understand these basic concepts because they will help you make informed decisions as an investor.

Let's look at an example to illustrate how the stock market works:

Example: Investing in a Bakery

Imagine Zenab, a 28-year-old passionate about baking who dreams of opening her bakery. She is well-known in her community for her delicious cakes and pastries. However, to start her bakery, Zenab needs 200,000 rupees but has saved only 100,000 rupees. Zenab approaches you, knowing that you love her pastries and believe in her baking talent. She asks if you would be willing to invest 100,000 rupees in exchange for a 50% bakery ownership. Seeing her potential and passion, you decide to invest.

The bakery opens, and just as expected, it's a hit! In three years, Zenab's business expands to three bakeries, each thriving. Since you own 50% of the business, your initial investment of 100,000 rupees has grown significantly, thanks to the bakery's success.

Look at a company's fundamentals before investing—earnings, growth, and management matter.

This scenario is similar to how the stock market operates. When you invest in a company by buying its stocks, you become a part-owner, sharing its profits and losses. The goal is to invest in companies that will grow over time, increasing the value of your stocks and allowing you to sell them for a profit.

The stock market offers a vast array of companies to invest in, ranging from those that produce everyday essentials to those that create cutting-edge technology. In India, we often say "Roti, Kapda, aur Makaan" (food, clothing, and shelter) are the three essentials for survival. The Indian stock market reflects this diversity, with companies in various sectors such as agriculture (wheat, rice, pulses), textiles (clothing, shoes), and construction (cement, steel, paints). No matter what industry you are interested in, the stock market likely has a company for you.

One of the most common questions people ask is, "Where is the stock market?" Unlike a traditional marketplace, the stock market isn't a physical location to walk around and see products. Instead, it exists through stock exchanges, which are virtual platforms where stocks are bought and sold.

In India, there are two major stock exchanges: the Bombay Stock Exchange

(BSE) in Mumbai and the National Stock Exchange (NSE) in Delhi. These exchanges are centralized hubs where traders and investors can buy and sell stocks. Other countries have their own stock exchanges, such as the New York Stock Exchange (NYSE) in the United States, the London Stock Exchange (LSE) in the United Kingdom, and the Tokyo Stock Exchange (TSE) in Japan. Each exchange provides a regulated environment where buyers and sellers can trade stocks and other financial securities.

You might wonder how people buy and sell stocks on these exchanges. Do you have to register directly with the BSE or NSE to start trading? The answer is no. Most people use intermediaries known as brokers to facilitate their trades.

Example: Real Estate vs. Stock Brokers

Think of it like buying a house. If Akash wants to buy a house in Noida, but he doesn't know much about the local real estate market, he might hire a real estate broker. The broker helps Akash find the right property, negotiates the price, and assists with all the paperwork. In this way, the broker makes the process of buying a house much easier and more efficient.

Similarly, in the stock market, a broker acts as an intermediary between you and the stock exchange. They provide a platform for you to buy and sell stocks, offer market insights, and may even give you investment advice based on your financial goals. Just like choosing the right real estate broker is crucial for buying a house, selecting a good stock broker is essential for a successful investing experience.

Investing in the stock market may seem intimidating initially, but with the right knowledge and tools, it can be a rewarding experience. By understanding the basics of stocks, how the market operates, and the role of brokers, you can start your journey toward becoming a confident investor.

Remember, every expert was once a beginner.

Take your time to learn, ask questions, and make informed decisions. The stock market is not just about making quick money; it's about growing your wealth over time by investing in businesses you believe in.

Let your money work for you, even when you're not.

My initial days

It all started in 2021, a year that marked the beginning of my journey into the world of investments. Before this, I had never taken the time to learn about the stock market or even think about where my money went beyond my basic expenses and savings. Like many people, I had heard a lot about the stock market—some good, some bad, and much of it confusing. It seemed like a place where people struck it rich or lost everything overnight. I had always considered it a complex world, a whole of jargon and technicalities that were beyond my understanding.

The stock market was painted as a high-stakes arena where only the brave or the foolish dared to venture. I remember hearing about how risky it was, how you needed to have a deep understanding of technical analysis, and how people who didn't know what they were doing could lose everything in a matter of hours. There was this perception that you had to be glued to multiple screens, constantly watching red and green lines, to have any chance of success. Movies and YouTube videos often showed people shouting at screens, sweating in front of stock tickers, and generally treating the stock market like a battlefield.

But the reality, as I found out, wasn't nearly as daunting. I am not a professional trader or a full-time investor, yet I have been able to make reasonable investments and earn decent returns. The truth is, you don't need to know everything or have a background in finance to start investing. There are many ways to begin that are simple and accessible, even for someone without any prior knowledge. This is something that not enough people talk about, and it's a shame because it keeps a lot of potential investors away.

My First Big Mistake: Looking back, one of the biggest mistakes I made was diving in without even a basic understanding of the market. I didn't know about exchanges, brokers, fees, or any of the fundamentals crucial to making informed decisions. In 2020, I was finishing my master's degree and landed a job, which came with a modest salary of 25,000 rupees per month. It wasn't much, but it was a start. When the COVID-19 pandemic hit, I, like many others, found myself stuck at home, with little opportunity to spend my earnings.

It was around this time that I first considered investing my money. My brother, who had a bit more experience, introduced me to the stock market and mentioned mutual funds as a good place to start. I asked him about the risks and how I should begin. At that point, I earned my own money and felt confident enough to invest 2,000 rupees. It wasn't a lot, but it was money that I was prepared to lose if things didn't go well. This was a crucial factor for me—I was investing my own money, so I didn't have to answer to anyone else if things went south.

So, in April 2021, I made my first investment: a one-time payment of 2,000 rupees in the Aditya Birla Sun Life Digital India Fund. The price per unit was around 105 rupees, and I managed to buy about 19 units. I remember how scared I was. I kept checking the fund's performance every few hours, not really knowing what I was looking for. I had no idea about holding periods, exit loads, or even what a fund manager was supposed to do.

A few days went by, and nothing much happened. I got busy with work and stopped obsessively checking the fund's performance. After a few weeks, I noticed that my investment had yielded a profit of

54 rupees. I was ecstatic! Without a second thought, I sold the units and pocketed my modest gain. It felt like a big win then, but in retrospect, I realize how much I lost by cashing out so early.

For some context, as of today, one unit of the same mutual fund is worth about 200 rupees. If I had held onto my investment, my initial 2,000 rupees would have almost doubled. Instead, I sold for a tiny profit and missed a much more significant gain. So, while I didn't technically lose money, I certainly lost out on a significant return. This experience taught me a valuable lesson: patience is key. The stock market rewards those who are willing to wait, and my premature sale was a perfect example of an opportunity missed.

After that initial foray into the market, I didn't invest for a few more months. When I did, it was once again in mutual funds, and I repeated the same mistake. I invested 5,000 rupees and sold again in a few weeks. At that point, I still didn't know much about individual stocks or how to evaluate them.

It wasn't until I started reading more and educating myself that I understood the potential of investing in individual companies.

I then joined as a researcher and started getting my fellowship. My fellowship was Rs 25000 monthly. Then I started venturing into Individual Stocks: In September 2021, I finally plunged into individual stocks. I bought one share of Tata Motors for about 333 rupees. This time, I was more patient. I waited and watched, and eventually sold the share for 490 rupees, making a profit of 160 rupees. That felt like a substantial gain—almost 50%

Don't buy a stock just because it's currently hot or in the news.

return on my initial investment. I was thrilled and felt like I was getting the hang of things. But as I've learned since then, a good start doesn't guarantee future success.

Reflecting on My Mistakes: Looking back, I realize that my early successes were more a result of luck than skill. While it's important to have a good first experience to build confidence, it's equally important to recognize that the stock market is unpredictable and that early gains can lead to overconfidence. After my initial wins, I felt emboldened and began making more investments, not all of which were as successful.

The Importance of Research: One of the most valuable lessons I learned was the importance of doing thorough research. In the beginning, I was relying on advice from my brother and random tips from friends. I wasn't taking the time to understand what I was investing in or why. This lack of knowledge left me vulnerable to making poor decisions. It was only after I started educating myself, reading articles, watching videos, and learning from more experienced investors that I began to make more informed choices. Another mistake I made was not understanding the value of holding onto investments. I was too focused on making quick profits, not realizing that some of the best returns come from holding onto good investments for the long term.

The stock market isn't a get-rich-quick scheme; it's a place where patience and informed decisions can lead to steady growth over time.

I also learned the hard way about the importance of diversification and risk management. Early on, I was putting all my money into a few investments, not realizing how risky that was. Over time, I learned to spread my investments across different sectors and asset classes, which helped to mitigate risk and provide more stable returns. The stock market can be volatile, and it's easy to panic when you see the value of your investments drop. In my early days, I would get anxious whenever there was a dip and sometimes made rash decisions. However, as I gained more experience, I learned that market fluctuations are normal and that it's important to stay calm and stick to your investment strategy.

One of the most challenging aspects of investing is managing emotions. It's easy to get swept up in the excitement of a booming market or to feel disheartened during a downturn. I've made my share of emotional decisions, and they often didn't end well. Over time, I've learned to keep my emotions in check and focus on the bigger picture. My journey in the stock market has been a continuous learning process. I've made mistakes, but I've also gained much knowledge and experience. I've learned that investing isn't just about making money; it's about understanding how the market works, managing risk, and making informed decisions. It's also about being patient and disciplined, sticking to your strategy, and not letting emotions dictate your actions.

For anyone just starting, my advice is to take it slow, do your research, and be prepared to learn from your mistakes. The stock market isn't as scary as it seems, and with time and effort, you can become a confident and successful investor. Remember, everyone makes mistakes, and that's okay. What's important is that you learn from them and keep moving forward.

Happy investing!

Is this the perfect time?

Absolutely, yes! If you are working and want to learn something new, then there is no better time than now. Whether you are in your twenties, thirties, or even fifties, it's never too late to start. The important thing is to make a start, no matter how small. The point isn't to risk a huge amount of money right away but to start with what you can comfortably afford—whether Rs. 100, Rs. 500 or Rs. 1000. This way, you can learn how investing works without putting yourself in financial jeopardy.

Think about this for a moment: Let's say you bought this book for some "X" amount (let's assume you paid Rs. 100). Now, try to invest in a way that allows you to earn that Rs. 100 back. Imagine you make that first Rs. 100 from your investment, and then it's like you got this book for free. It's a small but powerful motivation to get you started. I encourage you to invest a small amount and maybe earn enough for an evening's snack or tea. As you sip that cup of tea or enjoy your snacks, think more about the potential of investing.

So, is this the perfect time? Absolutely yes! I emphasize the importance of earning your own money because it's crucial to understand that you should never experiment with someone else's money. If you are not working and are considering borrowing money from someone to invest, I wouldn't recommend it. Although people do it, it comes with significant risks. The stock

Trying to time the market is risky, even for experts. Invest regularly and don't wait for the 'perfect' time.

market is not a guaranteed win, and there's always a chance you could lose money. It's better to risk your own money, even if it's just a small amount like Rs. 100 or Rs. 500 at first.

This is something that I believe everyone should know. There are many advantages to starting small and learning as you go. The more you learn, the better you get at making investment decisions. And remember, you don't need much money to start investing. These days, when I look around, I notice people are earning more compared to what people earned decades ago. This is a good thing because it means there is more potential to save and invest. However, I also see that people are spending more. While enjoying life and spending on things that make you happy is important, it's equally important to think about the future. I've noticed that only a small fraction of people invest, and most of them already have a good amount of capital. Those who earn Rs. 15,000 or Rs. 20,000 often think the stock market isn't for them. But that's not true!

The aim of this book is to encourage you to invest, regardless of your income level. Even if you start small, the key is to start. The earlier you begin, the more time your money has to grow. A person in their twenties or thirties has more time to take risks than someone in their fifties or sixties. Let's look at this with a simple example.

Imagine you enter a room with two people: Maan and Atul. Maan is 26 years old, and Atul is 52 years old. Maan has just started his career, while Atul is nearing retirement. Now, if I had to convince both of them to invest in the stock market, who do you think would be more likely to take the risk and try something new? It would probably be easier to convince Maan than Atul. Atul, being older, might have a substantial amount saved in his bank account. He might be more cautious because he is closer to retirement and doesn't want to risk losing his savings.

On the other hand, Maan is young and has just started earning. He has more time to recover from any potential losses, so he might be more willing to take risks and explore the stock market. This example shows that the younger you are, the more flexibility you have to experiment and learn. However, it doesn't mean older people shouldn't invest.

They just need to be more strategic and perhaps look for safer investment options.

One of the major mistakes I made during my initial investing days was not giving my

During your early days, focus on learning, and don't rush into making large investments. Gaining experience through small investments will help you understand market movements.

investments enough time to grow. In the

stock market and other investments, time is a crucial factor. The concept of time in investing is tied closely to the idea of compounding, where the returns you earn on your investments start earning returns themselves. The longer you leave your money invested, the more significant this compounding effect becomes.

Let's break down a few basic rules for anyone starting their investment journey:

Rule 1: Always play it safe at the beginning and take it slow.

Rule 2: Have patience. Investments often take time to grow and turn profitable.

Rule 3: Stay away from complicated investments that you don't understand.

These rules might sound simple, but trust me, they are very important. I didn't follow these principles when I started, and I made several mistakes because of it. I avoided overly complex investments, but I also didn't stick to safe options.

Another critical point to remember is that investing is not about timing the market but rather about the time you spend there. Many new investors make the mistake of trying to predict when the market will go up or down. However, even seasoned investors often find it difficult to time the market perfectly. Instead, focus on staying invested for the long term. By holding your investments over a longer period, you can ride out the ups and downs of the market and potentially benefit from its long-term growth.

Investing also has an emotional side. It's easy to get excited when the market is doing well and panic when it's not. The key is to stay calm and avoid making impulsive decisions based on short-term market movements. Stick to your investment plan, stay focused on your long-term goals, and remember why you started investing in the first place. If you're still unsure about starting your investment journey, look into it. Do your research, ask questions, and learn as much as possible. The more informed you are, the better your investment decisions will be.

And remember, every successful investor starts with their first investment.

I hope this book helps you take that first step toward investing. It doesn't matter how much you start with; what matters is that you start. The investing journey is full of learning and growth, and the earlier you begin, the more you stand to gain. So, what are you waiting for? Start small, learn as you go, and watch your money grow. You won't regret it.

Happy investing!

Why should you even care about investment?

Investing is a concept that can seem daunting, especially for those who are just starting their financial journey. When we think of investments, terms like stocks, bonds, and mutual funds can appear complex and intimidating. However, understanding why investment is important can simplify this process and make it accessible, even for those who are new to it. This chapter aims to shed light on the significance of investing, particularly for young or early-age investors, and to illustrate why it should be a crucial part of your financial planning.

At its core, investing is about making your money work for you. Instead of letting your savings sit idle, investments have the potential to grow and increase your wealth over time. Here's why investing should be a priority:

The Power of Compound Interest

One of the most compelling reasons to invest is the power of compound interest. This concept can be described simply: it's the process where the money you earn on your investment (interest or dividends) also earns money over time. The longer your money stays invested, the more it can grow. For instance, if you invest ₹10,000 in a savings account with an annual interest rate of 5%, you'll earn ₹500 in the first year. In the second year, you'll earn interest on ₹10,500, not just ₹10,000. Over the years, this compounding effect can lead to significant growth in your initial investment.

Let's consider an example. Suppose you invest ₹1,000 monthly in a mutual fund with an average annual return of 12%. After 20 years, your investment would grow to approximately ₹9,70,000. This growth is largely due to the compounding effect, which magnifies your returns as time progresses.

Beating Inflation

Inflation is the rate at which the general level of prices for goods and services rises, eroding purchasing power. If your money is just sitting in a savings account with a low interest rate, its value diminishes over time due to inflation.

The sooner you start, the better— compounding works best with time

For example, if inflation is at 6% annually and your savings account offers only 3% interest, your real purchasing power decreases by 3% yearly. Investing in assets like equities or real estate often provides returns that outpace inflation, helping you preserve and grow your purchasing power. Over time, investments like stocks or property have historically offered higher returns than inflation, ensuring that your money maintains its value.

Achieving Financial Goals

Investments are crucial for achieving long-term financial goals. Whether it's buying a home, funding education, or planning for retirement, having investments helps you reach these goals faster and more efficiently. For example, if you plan to buy a house in 10 years, saving a fixed amount monthly in a high-return investment could make this goal more attainable compared to traditional savings methods.

Let's illustrate this with a scenario. Imagine you want to save ₹10 lakhs for a down payment on a house in 10 years. If you save ₹5,000 monthly in a savings account with a 4% annual interest rate, you'll accumulate approximately ₹8.8 lakhs. However, if you invest the same amount in a mutual fund with an 12% annual return, you'll end up with about ₹20 lakhs, surpassing your target.

Building Wealth Over Time

Investing allows you to build wealth progressively. Unlike a savings account, which offers modest returns, investments can grow significantly over time. For instance, investing in high-growth stocks or diversified mutual funds can lead to substantial wealth accumulation. Warren Buffett, one of the most successful investors, has demonstrated how long-term investing can lead to enormous financial gains. Starting early and investing regularly helps you benefit from the long-term growth of the market, which can result in significant wealth accumulation.

Consider the example of an individual who starts investing ₹2,000 a month at the age of 25 in a diversified equity fund with an annual return of 14%. By the age of 65, this person could accumulate over ₹3 crores, thanks to the compounding effect and long-term growth of their investments.

Financial Independence and Security

Investing is a key step towards achieving financial independence and security. It allows you to build a financial cushion that can provide you with the freedom to pursue your passions, retire comfortably, or handle unforeseen expenses. Financial independence means having enough assets to support your lifestyle without relying solely on employment income. By investing wisely, you create a stream of passive income and build a safety net that provides you with greater control over your financial future.

For example, investing in dividend-paying stocks or real estate can generate a steady income stream that can cover your living expenses and provide financial security. Companies like ITC and Hindustan Unilever, known for their reliable dividends, can be part of a portfolio that supports long-term financial goals and independence.

Examples of Successful Investments: Learning from Real-Life Stories

To make the concept of investing more relatable, let's look at some real-life examples of companies and individuals who have benefited from investing over time. Please note that it is just for example and I nowhere intend to promote anything.

1. Reliance Industries Limited (RIL)

Reliance Industries, one of India's largest conglomerates, offers a compelling example of investment success. RIL's stock price has experienced substantial growth over the past decade, driven by its diversification into technology and

**Market downturns are like sales—
Buy quality stocks at a discount**

telecommunications. The launch of Jio, its telecom arm, revolutionized the Indian market and led to significant stock appreciation. Investors who bought RIL shares in 2015 saw their investment grow more than fivefold by 2023, showcasing the potential for long-term gains in the equity market.

2. HDFC Bank

HDFC Bank, a leading private sector bank in India, has consistently delivered strong financial performance and stock growth. Investors who purchased HDFC Bank shares a decade ago have enjoyed impressive returns, thanks to the bank's robust business model and steady growth. From ₹300 per share in 2013, the price has soared to over ₹3,000 in 2023, reflecting the bank's solid performance and investor confidence.

3. Bajaj Finance

Bajaj Finance, a non-banking financial company, is another example of investment success. Known for its rapid growth and innovative financial products,

Bajaj Finance has seen its stock price rise significantly over the past few years. Investors who bought shares in 2015 have seen their investments increase multiple times, illustrating the potential for high returns in the financial sector.

While tempting, penny stocks are highly volatile and risky for beginners. Always invest in companies with strong fundamentals and potential for growth.

Investing in equities offers several advantages and disadvantages crucial for potential investors to understand. One of the primary benefits is the potential for higher returns. Historically, equities have outperformed traditional savings methods, such as fixed deposits and savings accounts, providing investors with the opportunity to achieve significant financial growth over time. In addition, owning shares in a company grants investors ownership and voting rights, allowing them to have a say in important company decisions, such as electing board members or approving major corporate actions. Many companies also offer regular dividends, which can serve as a source of passive income, making equities an attractive option for those seeking steady returns. Furthermore, shares are highly liquid assets, meaning they can be bought or sold relatively quickly, providing investors with flexibility and the ability to respond to market changes or personal financial needs. Diversification is another advantage, as investing in a variety of sectors and asset classes can reduce overall risk and enhance portfolio stability.

However, there are also notable disadvantages to equity investing. Stock prices can be volatile, resulting in potential short-term losses that may be unsettling for some investors. Additionally, market risk is inherent in equities, with broad market movements potentially affecting individual investments. Unlike fixed-income investments, such as bonds or savings accounts, equities do not offer guaranteed returns, which means there is a risk of losing the initial investment if the company underperforms.

Investing in equities also requires a certain level of complexity; understanding market trends, analyzing company performance, and making informed decisions necessitates effort and knowledge. Moreover, market fluctuations can lead to emotional decision-making, where investors might react impulsively to short-term market changes, potentially impacting their long-term investment outcomes. Investing is a powerful tool for building wealth, achieving financial goals, and securing your future. By starting early and understanding the fundamentals of investing, you can benefit from the power of compounding, beat inflation, and build a strong financial foundation. While investing involves risks, the potential rewards make it a worthwhile endeavor. By learning from real-life examples and adopting a disciplined approach, you can navigate the world of investments and make informed decisions that align with your financial aspirations.

Investing is not just for the wealthy or experienced; it's a crucial part of financial planning for everyone, including young and early-age investors. Embrace the journey, stay informed, and watch your investments grow over time.

What if you think it is still risky?

It is our very basic human tendency to consider the possible risks before putting our hard-earned money into something. And it should be considered. A person who does not consider the positives as well as the negatives before risking their money is careless. For a person like me, I will always consider the possible risks first before even looking into anything. And it must hold true for several reasons.

Let us consider an example- Anil is a 26-year-old researcher. He gets his fellowship every month, saving around 20,000 from it every month. He was informed by a fellow friend to start investing. That fellow friend introduced him to a mutual fund and asked him to pay 15,000 every month and promised him that after 5 years, he would get decent returns (Considering the figure anil invested and expecting a return of 12%, the invested amount will be 9,00,000 and the total return will be around 12,37,000). Now, he has started the mutual fund and is paying a regular SIP of 15,000. After 8 months, he wanted to check his portfolio. He contacted his friend, who further asked the bank or the mutual fund provider and then reverted the amount.

Now, let us assume after 2 years, due to some emergency, he wanted to take his investment out. Let us assume he does not wish to continue investing. Then what? What if after 5 months, he wants to start again? Is it all possible?

To answer that question, let me introduce something called Mutual funds. With numerous investment options available, ranging from stocks and bonds to real estate and commodities, it's easy to feel overwhelmed. However, one investment vehicle that stands out for early investors due to its simplicity, diversification, and potential for growth is mutual funds. Understanding what mutual funds are and the advantages they offer can help clarify the investment process and provide a solid foundation for building wealth over time.

A mutual fund is an investment vehicle that pools money from multiple investors to purchase a diversified portfolio of securities, such as stocks, bonds, or a combination of both. Managed by professional fund managers, mutual funds aim to achieve specific investment objectives, whether that's growth, income, or a balanced mix of both. By investing in mutual funds, even those with limited knowledge or funds can participate in the financial markets.

Let us explain it with another simple example- Priti is a school teacher. She is the only earning member in a family of 3. She earns around 40,000 per month, and she manages to save 5000 per month after all her expenses. Now, she wants to invest in something that is very safe and also not that complicated. A friend of hers suggests mutual funds. But why a mutual fund?

In a mutual fund, the risk is lessened because the investment is spread across a wide range of securities. If one security performs poorly, the impact on the overall portfolio is minimized, as it is likely offset by the performance of other securities in the fund. This makes mutual funds a less risky investment option than purchasing individual stocks or bonds, where the performance of a single security can significantly impact the investor's return.

Managing investments requires expertise, time, and access to information, which many early investors may not have. Mutual funds are managed by experienced professionals who conduct thorough research and analysis before making investment decisions. These fund managers continuously monitor market conditions and adjust the portfolio to align with the fund's investment objectives. This professional management provides a level of oversight and strategic decision-making that individual investors might find challenging to achieve on their own. Liquidity is another compelling advantage of mutual funds. Liquidity refers to the ease with which an asset can be converted into cash without affecting its market price. Mutual funds are generally highly liquid investments because they can be bought or sold on any business day at the fund's net asset value (NAV). This means investors can access their money relatively quickly in times of need, unlike some other investment options that may have longer holding periods or higher transaction costs. The ability to buy and sell mutual funds with ease makes them a convenient option for early investors who may need access to their funds.

Additionally, mutual funds offer a wide variety of investment options to cater to different financial goals and risk tolerances.

Mutual fund investments are best suited for long-term growth. Avoid the temptation to make frequent changes to your portfolio based on short-term market fluctuations.

There are equity funds, which invest primarily in stocks and aim for capital appreciation; bond funds, which focus on generating income through investments in bonds; balanced funds, which provide a mix of stocks and bonds for both growth and income; and index funds, which aim to replicate the performance of a specific market index, such as the S&P 500. This variety allows early investors to choose a fund that aligns with their financial objectives, whether they are looking for long-term growth, income generation, or a combination of both.

Mutual funds also offer transparency and regulatory oversight, providing a sense of security to early investors. In many countries, mutual funds are required to adhere to strict regulatory standards that govern their operations, disclosure, and reporting. Fund managers must provide regular updates on the fund's performance, holdings, and fees, which are disclosed in a fund's prospectus and annual reports. This transparency ensures that investors are well-informed about where their money is going and how it is being managed. Furthermore, the regulatory oversight helps protect investors from fraudulent activities, making mutual funds a safer investment choice.

For early investors, mutual funds also provide an excellent opportunity to participate in the financial markets with relatively low initial investments. Unlike other investment options that might require a significant amount of capital, many mutual funds have low minimum investment requirements with as low as 100 rupees SIP per month. This accessibility makes mutual funds a great starting point for those who are just beginning their investment journey. It allows them to start investing with small amounts of money and gradually build their portfolio as they gain confidence and knowledge.

If you are someone who wants to start his/her investment journey and do not wish to risk your money, then a mutual fund is one such great option to start. With this comes another important question- Are all mutual funds good? Can we blindly invest in any mutual fund if it has so many advantages?

The answer to these questions are a big "No." You should never invest into something blindly. There are few mutual funds that you can choose, we can discuss about it later towards the end.

Is there any other safe way to invest if not mutual fund?

Yes, there are several options that you can explore and start your investment journey. Let us discuss some of them in the next few pages.

?
BANK
BANK FD
RD
PPF
REAL ESTATE
STOCKS
GOLD
GOLD
REAL ESATE
STOCKS
PPF
MUTAL FUNDS

Other investment options

Investing can seem like a daunting task, especially for beginners. With so many options available, it can be overwhelming to decide where to start. However, understanding the various investment avenues is crucial for making informed decisions that align with your financial goals and risk tolerance. Each investment option comes with its own set of advantages and disadvantages, and what works for one person may not necessarily be suitable for another.

Mutual funds, for example, are often considered an ideal starting point for first-time investors. They offer a relatively low-risk way to enter the market, allowing individuals to start with a minimal amount of capital—sometimes as little as 100 rupees. Mutual funds pool money from many investors to purchase a diversified portfolio of stocks, bonds, or other securities, which helps to spread out risk and provides the benefit of professional management. For those who are new to investing and may not have the time or expertise to manage individual investments, mutual funds can be an excellent choice.

But what if you're ready to explore other investment opportunities beyond mutual funds? There are several alternatives, each with its own set of characteristics, potential returns, and risks. In this chapter, we will delve into some of the most common investment options, including Fixed Deposits (FDs), Systematic Deposits (SDs), PPFs, equities, real estate, gold, and bonds. We will discuss the benefits and drawbacks of each, helping you to better understand which options might suit your financial needs and objectives.

Bank Fixed Deposits (FDs)

FDs are one of the simplest and most secure investment options available in India. They involve depositing a lump sum amount with a bank for a fixed period at a predetermined interest rate. FDs are highly favored for their guaranteed returns and low risk. When you open an FD, you deposit a specific amount of money with a bank for a fixed term, which can range from a few months to several years. The bank offers a fixed interest rate on this deposit, which does not change during the term of the FD. At the end of the term, you receive the principal amount along with the interest earned.

For example, if you invest ₹1 lakh in an FD with an interest rate of 6% per annum for 1 year, you will receive ₹1 lakh + ₹6,000 (interest) = ₹1,06,000 at maturity.

FDs are considered low-risk investments because they offer guaranteed returns. The principal amount is protected, and the interest rate is fixed. Furthermore, deposits up to ₹5 lakh per bank are insured by the Deposit Insurance and Credit Guarantee Corporation (DICGC), adding an extra layer of safety. FDs are ideal for conservative investors who prioritize safety and guaranteed returns. They are particularly suitable for retirees, individuals looking to save for short-term goals, and those who prefer a fixed and secure return on their investment.

There are several advantages, some of them are:

Guaranteed Returns: The interest rate is fixed, so you know exactly how much you will earn.

Safety: The principal and interest are secure, with insurance up to ₹5 lakh.

Flexibility: You can choose the term of the FD based on your needs.

Ease of Management: Easy to open and manage through banks.

Disadvantages of fixed deposits.

Lower Returns: FD returns are generally lower compared to other investment options like stocks or mutual funds.

Taxation: Interest earned is fully taxable, which can reduce the effective return.

Early Withdrawal Penalties: Withdrawing funds before maturity usually incurs a penalty and reduces interest earned.

Recurring deposits (RDs)

Another investment option similar to fixed deposit is Recurring Deposits (RDs). Recurring Deposits (RDs) are a type of fixed deposit that allows individuals to invest a fixed amount every month for a predetermined period. RDs are a good option for those who want to save regularly and earn interest on their savings.

With an RD, you deposit a fixed amount of money every month into an RD account for a specified period. The interest rate is similar to that of FDs, and the amount deposited each month earns interest. At the end of the term, you receive the total amount deposited plus the interest earned.

For instance, if you invest ₹2,000 monthly for 1 year in an RD with an interest rate of 6% per annum, you will receive the sum of all your monthly deposits along with the interest accrued.

RDS are low-risk investments, similar to FDs, as the interest rate is fixed and guaranteed. The principal amount is safe, and interest is earned at a guaranteed rate. RDs are suitable for individuals who want to save a fixed amount regularly and earn interest on it. They are ideal for people with a steady monthly income and those who want to build savings for short- to medium-term goals.

Public Provident Fund (PPF)

The Public Provident Fund (PPF) is a government-backed savings scheme designed to encourage long-term savings among Indian citizens. It offers tax benefits and a fixed return on investment. To invest in a PPF, you open an account with a bank or post office. You can invest a minimum of ₹500 and a maximum of ₹1.5 lakh in a financial year. The government sets the interest rate, which is compounded annually. The PPF account has a lock-in period of 15 years, but it can be extended in blocks of 5 years after maturity.

For example, if you invest ₹1 lakh per year for 15 years in a PPF with an interest rate of 7.1% per annum, you will receive the total deposit amount plus the compounded interest earned over the period.

PPF is considered a low-risk investment due to government backing. The interest rate is guaranteed, and the principal amount is secure. PPF is suitable for individuals looking for a safe, long-term investment with tax benefits. It is ideal for those saving for retirement, children's education, or other long-term financial goals. There are several advantages of PPF, some of them are:

Safety: Backed by the government, making it a secure investment.

Tax Benefits: Contributions are eligible for tax deductions under Section 80C, and interest earned is tax-free.

Attractive Returns: Generally offers higher returns than traditional savings accounts.

Long-Term Growth: Encourages long-term savings with a 15-year lock-in period.

Equity Shares (Stocks)

Equity shares, or stocks, represent ownership in a company. When you buy shares of a company, you own a portion of that company and have a claim on its profits and assets. Investing in equity shares involves buying shares of a company at the current market price. The value of these shares can fluctuate based on the company's performance, market conditions, and economic factors. Investors can earn returns through capital appreciation (increase in share price) and dividends (a portion of the company's profits distributed to shareholders).

For example, if you buy 100 shares of a company at ₹100 per share and the price rises to ₹150, you can sell the shares for a profit of ₹5,000 (100 shares x ₹50 increase per share).

Risk Level: Equity shares carry a high-risk level due to market volatility. The value of shares can fluctuate widely, and there is a risk of losing the entire investment if the company performs poorly.

Equity shares are suitable for investors who are willing to take higher risks for potentially higher returns. They are ideal for individuals with a long-term investment horizon, a good understanding of the stock market, and a higher risk tolerance.

Some of the advantages includes:

Potential for High Returns: Equity shares offer the potential for significant capital appreciation and dividends.

Ownership: Shareholders have ownership in the company and may have voting rights.

Liquidity: Shares can be bought and sold on stock exchanges, providing liquidity.

Diversification: Investors can diversify their portfolio by investing in various companies and sectors.

Avoid taking loans or borrowing money to invest as a beginner; the risk is too high.

Disadvantages:

High Risk: Shares are subject to market risks and fluctuations, which can lead to losses.

Requires Knowledge: Successful investing in stocks requires research and understanding of the market.

No Guaranteed Returns: Unlike fixed-income investments, there are no guaranteed returns.

Bonds

Bonds are fixed-income securities where you lend money to an issuer (government or corporation) in exchange for periodic interest payments and the return of the principal amount at maturity. Bonds are used by investors seeking steady income with lower risk compared to equities.

When you invest in a bond, you purchase it from the issuer at a fixed price. The issuer pays you interest at regular intervals (usually semi-annually or annually) and returns the principal amount at the end of the bond's term. There are various types of bonds, including government bonds, corporate bonds, and municipal bonds.

For example, if you buy a ₹1 lakh government bond with a 7% annual interest rate for 10 years, you will receive ₹7,000 annually as interest and get back the ₹1 lakh principal at maturity.

Bonds generally have a low to moderate risk level. Government bonds are considered low-risk, while corporate bonds carry more risk depending on the issuer's creditworthiness. Bonds are suitable for investors looking for steady income and lower risk compared to stocks. They are ideal for conservative investors, retirees, and those seeking capital preservation and regular interest payments.

Advantages:

Steady Income: Regular interest payments provide predictable income.

Lower Risk: Government bonds are low-risk; corporate bonds vary based on credit rating.

Predictable Returns: Fixed interest payments and principal return if held to maturity.

Diversification: Adds stability and diversification to an investment portfolio.

Disadvantages:

Lower Returns: Generally lower returns compared to equities.

Taxation: Interest income is taxable, reducing effective returns.

Interest Rate Risk: Bond prices can fall if interest rates rise.

Less Liquidity: Bonds may be less liquid compared to stocks or mutual funds.

Real Estate

Investing in real estate involves purchasing property (residential, commercial, or land) to earn rental income and benefit from capital appreciation. Real estate can be a tangible asset offering diversification in an investment portfolio.

When you invest in real estate, you buy property with the aim of earning rental income and/or selling it at a higher price in the future. You can invest in residential properties (homes, apartments), commercial properties (offices, retail spaces), or land. You can also invest indirectly in real estate through Real Estate Investment Trusts (REITs).

For example, if you buy an apartment for ₹50 lakh and rent it out for ₹20,000 per month, you earn ₹2.4 lakh annually as rental income. Additionally, if the property's value appreciates over time, you can sell it for a profit.

Real estate investments carry a moderate to high-risk level. Property values can fluctuate based on market conditions, economic factors, and location. There are also risks related to property management, tenant issues, and maintenance costs.

Real estate is suitable for investors with significant capital who are looking for long-term investments. It is ideal for those who are comfortable with the illiquidity and market risks associated with property investments and seek diversification.

There are few advantages of investing here:

Rental Income: Potential for steady income through rent.

Capital Appreciation: Potential for property value increase over time.

Tangible Asset: Provides a sense of security and ownership.

Diversification: Adds diversity to an investment portfolio.

Disadvantages:

High Initial Investment: Requires significant capital for purchasing property.

Illiquidity: Selling a property can be time-consuming and costly.

Market Fluctuations: Property values can be affected by market and economic conditions.

Gold and Precious Metals

Investing in gold and precious metals involves purchasing physical gold, gold ETFs, sovereign gold bonds, or other precious metals like silver and platinum. Gold is often considered a safe-haven asset and a hedge against inflation and economic uncertainty.

Gold investments can be made through various methods:

Physical Gold: Buying gold jewelry, coins, or bars.

Gold ETFs: Exchange-Traded Funds that track the price of gold and are traded on stock exchanges.

Sovereign Gold Bonds (SGBs): Government-issued bonds representing gold, offering periodic interest payments.

Digital Gold: Buying gold through online platforms that allow fractional investments.

For example, if you invest in a Gold ETF, the value of your investment will track the price of gold. If the price of gold rises, the value of your ETF investment will also increase.

Risk Level: The risk level of gold investments varies. Physical gold involves storage and security risks, while gold ETFs and SGBs are affected by gold price fluctuations but generally offer lower risk compared to equities. Gold investments are suitable for individuals looking for a hedge against inflation and economic uncertainty. They are ideal for those seeking diversification and a safe-haven investment.

When it comes to investing, one thing is clear: there is no one-size-fits-all approach. Each person has unique financial goals, risk tolerance, and investment preferences, which means that the type of investment that works best can vary widely from one individual to another. For some, the idea of putting money into a savings account might seem like the most secure and reliable option. And that's perfectly fine—everyone has their own comfort level when it comes to managing their finances.

However, it's important to understand that even the money sitting in your savings account isn't just lying dormant. Banks don't simply hold onto your cash; they invest it in various financial instruments to earn returns. In essence, your money is already being used in different investment options, though you might not see direct returns on these investments.

As you start exploring new investment opportunities, especially those that involve a degree of risk, it's crucial to be diligent and cautious. Investing isn't just about putting your money into something and hoping for the best. It requires careful consideration and understanding of what you're getting into. You've probably heard the phrase, "Investments in securities are subject to market risks. Please read all documents carefully before investing." This isn't just a throwaway line—it's a critical reminder of the uncertainties that come with investing.

The reason for this cautionary advice is simple: nothing in the investment world is guaranteed. The stock market, for example, can be highly volatile, with prices fluctuating based on a multitude of factors, from economic news to company performance. There are no sure things, and even the most seemingly stable investments can carry risk. This is why it's so important to do your homework, understand the risks involved, and make informed decisions that align with your financial goals and risk tolerance.

In the end, the best investment is the one that makes you feel confident and secure, knowing that you've made the right choice for your financial future. Whether that's keeping your money in a savings account, diving into stocks, or exploring other financial instruments, what's most important is that you're aware of your options and the potential risks and rewards associated with each. By taking a thoughtful and measured approach, you can navigate the world of investing with greater confidence and peace of mind.

Equity investments provide ownership in a company. When the company grows, so does the value of your shares.

Understanding investment in equity

As we have discussed the various aspects of investing, it's time to introduce a very important and intriguing concept called the "Dividend." For me, the idea of dividends was a major inspiration to start conversations about the advantages of investing. The more I learned, the more I realized that many people earn a substantial amount of money purely from dividends. In fact, for some investors, dividends are a key factor when deciding where to invest their money.

But what exactly is a dividend? In simple terms, I would describe it as a "reward." A dividend is essentially a reward you receive for having faith in a particular company. It is a portion of the company's profits that is distributed to its shareholders. When you own shares in a company, you are entitled to a share of its profits, and dividends are one way the company can share its success with you.

To illustrate this, let's consider an example.

Imagine Monika, a 29-year-old housewife who manages her household with a family of four. Monika regularly goes grocery shopping and loves cooking. She is very particular about the brands she uses in her kitchen—for instance, she always buys rice and cooking oil from specific brands that she trusts.

Over time, Monika notices that many of the grocery items she buys come from the same parent company. She has a high level of trust in this company because its products are consistently of good quality and are always in stock at her local grocery store. She believes that the company produces safe and reliable food products. Now, if someone were to ask Monika which company she thinks has a strong potential for growth in the fast-moving consumer goods (FMCG) sector, she would likely mention the brand she regularly uses. She believes in the quality of its products and has seen firsthand how well they sell in stores.

If Monika were to invest in this company by purchasing its shares, she would become a shareholder. If the company performs well and generates profits, it might decide to share a portion of those profits with its shareholders in the form of dividends. Monika would then receive dividends as a reward for her belief in the company's success and for being a part of its growth journey.

This is the essence of dividends: they are a way for companies to share their success with the people who have invested in them. For investors like Monika, dividends can provide a steady income stream in addition to any potential gains from the increase in the value of the company's shares. For many, the prospect of earning dividends is a compelling reason to invest in equities, making it an integral part of their investment strategy.

Investing in equities offers a promising avenue for wealth creation, but it also comes with its share of risks. To maximize returns and minimize potential losses, it is essential to adopt a strategic approach.

Here are some detailed guidelines to consider for reducing risk and enhancing investment outcomes in the stock market as a beginner:

1. Invest in Large-Cap Companies with Strong Fundamentals

When entering the stock market, one prudent strategy is to focus on large-cap companies with solid fundamentals. Large-cap companies, typically defined as those with a market capitalization of over ₹10,000 crore, are generally more stable and less volatile than their smaller counterparts. These companies often have a well-established market presence, robust financial health, and a track record of consistent performance.

Investing in large-cap companies allows you to benefit from their stability and growth potential. Look for companies with strong fundamentals, such as a healthy balance sheet, consistent revenue and profit growth, and effective management. Analyze financial statements, profit margins, debt levels, and cash flow to ensure that the company is well-positioned to withstand market fluctuations. For instance, companies like Reliance Industries, HDFC Bank, and Tata Consultancy Services have demonstrated resilience and growth over time, making them attractive options for conservative investors seeking stability and long-term appreciation.

2. Avoid Investing Money Needed in the Short-Term

Another crucial principle of equity investing is to avoid putting in money that you might need in the near future, typically within the next six months. The stock market can be volatile in the short term, with prices fluctuating due to various factors, including economic conditions, market sentiment, and company-specific news. By investing funds that you might need in the immediate future, you expose yourself to the risk of having to sell your investments at an inopportune time, potentially at a loss.

To mitigate this risk, allocate only surplus funds to equity investments—money that you can afford to leave invested for a longer period. This approach allows you to weather market downturns and benefit from the long-term growth potential of equities. By maintaining an emergency fund and keeping your short-term financial needs separate from your investment capital, you can avoid the pressure of prematurely liquidating investments.

3. Exercise Patience and Focus on Major Players

Patience is a key virtue in equity investing. The stock market often requires time for investments to appreciate and for the benefits of your decisions to materialize. It is essential to have a long-term perspective and avoid making impulsive decisions based on short-term market movements. Instead of reacting to daily price fluctuations, focus on the overall growth trajectory of your investments.

Investing in significant players within a sector can be a wise strategy. Companies with a significant market share or are leaders in their industry tend to have a competitive advantage and a higher probability of sustained success. For example, investing in a significant player in the technology sector like Infosys or a leading FMCG company like Hindustan Unilever can provide exposure to robust market trends and growth opportunities. These companies often have the resources and expertise to navigate economic challenges and capitalize on emerging trends, making them more likely to deliver favorable returns over the long term.

By following these principles—investing in large-cap companies with strong fundamentals, avoiding the funds needed in the short term, and exercising patience while focusing on significant players—you can enhance your chances of achieving positive outcomes in equity investing. While no investment is without risk, adopting a disciplined and informed approach can help you navigate the complexities of the stock market and work towards achieving your financial goals.

Freedom of control

Investing is a powerful tool for building wealth, but it can often feel uncertain. Markets go up and down, economies shift, and sometimes individual companies experience unexpected challenges. This unpredictability makes it hard to always know what's coming next, which is why taking control of your investments is so important. Without control, you may feel lost or uncertain. But with control, you gain security and the freedom to manage your financial future.

Let's break this down with a real-life example. Imagine I regularly invest ₹15,000 every month through a Systematic Investment Plan (SIP). After 2 years, I suddenly needed ₹80,000 for an emergency. The questions that immediately came to mind were:

Can I withdraw my money whenever I need it?

What happens if I skip a few months of SIP because I don't have extra cash?

If I have more money, can I add it to my SIP?

Will I face penalties for not contributing on time?

These are common concerns that all investors have. They highlight the importance of having control over your money. It's your hard-earned cash, and you should be able to manage it according to your needs. Control over your investments doesn't just give you security—it also gives you the freedom to make choices that align with your financial goals. In this chapter, we'll discuss how taking control of your portfolio empowers you, giving you both peace of mind and flexibility.

1. Why Controlling Your Investments Is Essential

For beginners, the world of investments can seem overwhelming. There are a lot of technical terms like "diversification," "asset allocation," and "portfolio management," which might seem complex. But at the heart of these concepts is the basic idea of control. Controlling your investments means understanding where your money is going, why you've chosen certain assets, and how your portfolio might perform over time.

Example: Let's say you invested in a mix of stocks and bonds. If you don't have control over your investments, you might not even know when one part of your portfolio is doing well or underperforming. Without control, you might miss opportunities to sell high or buy more when prices are low. Being in control means you can navigate these situations better, make informed decisions, and ultimately protect your wealth.

The Connection Between Control and Security: Having control over your investments helps you weather financial ups and downs. Markets are always fluctuating, and it's hard to avoid downturns. However, when you know where your money is and why it's there, you can stay calm during turbulent times. Instead of reacting out of fear, you're able to act rationally and based on your overall strategy.

For instance, during a market crash, some people panic and sell everything. But if you have control, you can look at the situation and determine whether you should hold on to your investments or even buy more at lower prices. This level of control doesn't just protect your portfolio from rash decisions—it can also lead to better financial outcomes in the long run.

Control Provides Freedom: Control over your investments doesn't just protect you from losses; it also gives you freedom. You have the power to choose how your money grows and how much risk you're comfortable taking on. You can adjust your strategy as your goals evolve, which offers you more flexibility than rigid investment plans or relying on someone else to make decisions for you.

For example, if you start a new job with a higher salary, you might decide to invest more aggressively. Or, if you're nearing retirement, you could shift to more conservative investments. Having control over your portfolio means you can make changes based on your life stage and personal preferences, rather than following a one-size-fits-all approach.

2. The Psychological Benefits of Controlling Your Investments

Many people focus on the financial aspects of investing, like returns and profits. But controlling your investments also provides psychological benefits. Feeling secure in your financial decisions and knowing that you have the power to manage your money can reduce stress and build confidence.

Example: Arjun's Investment Journey

Arjun worked as a technician at a university, where he had plenty of time to monitor his stock investments. He regularly bought and sold stocks based on market trends. However, after three years, Arjun switched to a demanding job, which left him with little time to manage his portfolio.

Rather than giving up on investing, Arjun chose to switch his investments to a mutual fund. Even though a fund manager now oversees the portfolio, Arjun still exercises control over his investment strategy. He has the freedom to choose the fund that aligns with his goals, and he can adjust his contributions as needed. This balance of control gave Arjun peace of mind during a busy period of his life.

Just like Arjun, being involved in every step of the investment process builds a sense of ownership. Whether your investments succeed or face challenges, you know that the outcome is influenced by your choices. This sense of responsibility leads to better decision-making. When you're in control, you're more likely to take time to research your options and make thoughtful decisions, which can ultimately lead to better financial outcomes.

Controlling Investments Reduces Stress: Market ups and downs can be stressful, especially for people who feel they have little control over their portfolios. Investors who leave their financial future entirely in the hands of others might experience higher levels of anxiety during turbulent times. However, if you're actively managing your investments and have a strategy in place, you're more likely to remain calm and see market dips as opportunities to buy low, rather than reasons to panic.

3. Why Flexibility is Crucial for Long-Term Success

Markets change, industries evolve, and companies face new challenges. To succeed in the long term, your investment strategy must be flexible. When you have control, you can make changes as necessary—whether it's adjusting your asset allocation or shifting to more promising opportunities. Without control, you risk sticking to outdated strategies or missing out on new growth opportunities.

Example: Consider someone who invested heavily in traditional retail stocks in the early 2000s. As e-commerce began to dominate, retail stocks began to struggle. An investor who was in control of their portfolio might have noticed this trend and moved their investments into e-commerce or tech stocks. Someone who wasn't paying attention or didn't have control might have missed out on this shift, losing out on potential gains.

4. Examples of Real-Life Investment Control

Let's look at a few more examples to understand how control plays a key role in investing:

Example 1: The 2008 Financial Crisis

The 2008 financial crisis was a wake-up call for many investors. People who didn't have control over their investments—either because they relied solely on a financial advisor or invested in rigid funds—suffered significant losses. On the other hand, those who actively managed their portfolios could make better decisions during the crisis. Some investors moved their money into safer assets like bonds or cash, while others took advantage of the lower stock prices to buy shares at a discount.

Example 2: Start-Up Investor's Strategy

An investor who focuses on start-ups needs to be very hands-on. Start-ups are volatile, and their stock prices can swing dramatically based on new product launches or funding rounds. An investor who stays involved and keeps an eye on market conditions can make timely decisions to either exit before a potential downturn or invest more during a promising growth phase.

Example: Imagine you invest all your money in a single tech company. If the company performs well, you may see significant gains. But what if a competitor introduces superior technology, causing the stock to drop? Your entire investment could be at risk. Conversely, if you diversify by also investing in sectors like healthcare, consumer goods, and bonds, poor performance in the tech sector will have less impact on your overall portfolio.

Control doesn't stop once you've set up a diversified portfolio. To maintain control, you must periodically rebalance your portfolio. Rebalancing involves adjusting your asset allocation to ensure that it stays aligned with your investment strategy.

Example: Let's say your goal is to keep 60% of your portfolio in stocks and 40% in bonds. After a year of strong stock market performance, your portfolio may now be 70% stocks and only 30% bonds. While this may seem like a good problem to have, it also means your portfolio is now riskier than you intended. Rebalancing allows you to sell some of your stocks and buy more bonds, restoring your original asset allocation.

The Role of Technology in Helping You Control Your Investments

In today's digital age, technology has made it easier than ever for investors to take control of their portfolios. From online brokerage platforms to mobile apps, there are countless tools available to help you manage your investments.

Online Brokers: Platforms like Zerodha, Groww, Angel One, Upstox, and many such platforms provide investors with the tools they need to buy and sell securities, monitor portfolio performance, and execute trades—all with a few clicks. This ease of access ensures that investors can stay on top of their portfolios without needing to rely on financial advisors.

Nowadays, it is very easy to start your investment journey. We will discuss in the last part of the book- "The One-year long experiment"

Let us take one final example: Warren Buffett's Investment Strategy

Warren Buffett is famous for his hands-on approach to investing. Rather than delegating decisions to a team of advisors, Buffett controls his own portfolio, conducting deep research into the companies he invests in. His investment strategy, often described as "buy and hold," involves choosing companies with strong fundamentals and holding them for the long term. Buffett's ability to control his investments, rather than following trends or relying on external advice, has been a key factor in his success.

The Risks of Not Controlling Your Investments: Just as control brings security and freedom, a lack of control can expose you to unnecessary risks. When you don't actively manage your investments, you may find yourself at the mercy of market trends, fees, and poor-performing assets.

Many investors delegate the management of their portfolios to financial advisors or invest in pre-packaged mutual funds. While this can save time, it often comes at the cost of higher fees and less personalization. Advisors may not always prioritize your best interests, and mutual funds may not align with your specific financial goals.

So it is very important for you as a beginner to decide and keep your financial goals clear.

The one-year-long experiment.

Disclaimer: I am not forcing you to start your investment by risking your money. Please invest wisely and always start with small capital.

Aim: The aim of this experiment is to introduce you to the world of investments through a safe and structured approach. By investing in a mutual multicap fund for one year, you will learn the basics of investing, understand the growth potential, and experience the benefits of disciplined investing without taking on excessive risk. This experiment is designed for beginners who have no prior experience in the stock market or investments.

Materials and Method

Materials Required:

Smartphone: A basic smartphone with internet access.

Internet Connection: A stable internet connection to download the app and perform transactions.

Investment Capital: A minimum amount of money to start with, such as ₹500 to ₹1,000. This is the money you will invest in the mutual fund.

Bank Account: A savings account linked with your investment app for easy transactions.

PAN Card and Aadhar Card: Essential documents for KYC (Know Your Customer) verification.

Method:

Choosing a Broker: A broker is a platform or an app that allows you to buy and sell mutual funds. Some popular brokers in India include Zerodha, Groww, Paytm Money, and Upstox. These brokers have user-friendly mobile apps that make it easy to invest even if you're a beginner.

Downloading the App: Go to the App Store (for iPhone users) or Play Store (for Android users). Search for the broker app of your choice, for example, "XYZ". Click on the "Install" button to download and install the app on your phone.

Registering on the App: Open the app after installation. You will be asked to create an account.

Enter your email address or mobile number and create a password. Verify your email or phone number by entering the OTP (One Time Password) sent to your device.

Complete the KYC (Know Your Customer) process by providing your PAN card, Aadhar card, and bank account details. This is a mandatory step as per government regulations.

Once your KYC is approved, your account will be ready to use.

Adding Money to Your Account: After registration, you need to add money to your account to start investing. Go to the "Add

Funds" or "Wallet" section of the app. Enter the amount you wish to invest (₹500, ₹1,000, or more). Choose your linked bank account and follow the instructions to transfer money into your investment account.

Selecting a Mutual Multicap Fund: Mutual funds pool money from various investors and invest in different financial assets like stocks and bonds. A multicap fund is a type of mutual fund that invests in companies of all sizes—large, medium, and small.

Go to the "Mutual Funds" section of the app.

Use the search bar to look for "Multicap Funds."

You will see a list of multicap funds with different past performances, risk levels, and fund managers.

Read the fund details, including the returns over the last 1 year, 3 years, and 5 years, the risk level, and the minimum investment amount. Select a fund that suits your risk appetite and has a good track record.

Starting Your Investment: Once you have selected a fund, click on the "Invest" button. Choose the investment amount (it can be a lump sum or a systematic investment plan (SIP) where a fixed amount is invested monthly). Review the order and confirm the investment.

Congratulations! You have successfully invested in a mutual multicap fund.

Principle: The principle behind this 1-year experiment is to help you understand the power of regular, disciplined investing. Mutual multicap funds are an ideal choice for beginners because they provide exposure to a diverse range of companies, which helps spread risk. By investing a small amount regularly over a year, you will not only learn how investments work but also develop the habit of saving and investing, which is crucial for building wealth over time.

This experiment teaches you the importance of patience and staying invested, as mutual fund returns can fluctuate in the short term but tend to perform better over the long term.

Monitor Your Investment: Check your app periodically to track the performance of your mutual fund. Remember, this experiment is about learning and staying invested for one year. Review After 1 Year: After one year, evaluate the growth of your investment. Consider whether you want to continue investing, withdraw, or make changes to your investment strategy.

Results

By following this experiment for one year, you will achieve several key outcomes:

Practical Investment Experience: You will gain hands-on experience in investing, understanding how to navigate a broker app, select a fund, and manage your investment.

Understanding of Mutual Funds: You will learn about mutual funds, specifically multicap funds, and their role in diversifying investments across different types of companies.

Growth in Investment: Assuming a moderate annual return, your investment should have grown over the year, providing a real-life example of how investments can outperform traditional savings accounts.

Financial Discipline: You will develop a habit of saving and investing, which is essential for building long-term wealth and financial security.

Awareness of Market Fluctuations: You will understand that investments can fluctuate in value and that staying invested for a longer term usually reduces risk and enhances returns.

By the end of this experiment, you will be better equipped to make informed financial decisions, understand the basics of investing, and appreciate the importance of regular, disciplined investment strategies.

Happy investing!!